THE ENTRANCE HALL

Visitors to Hopetoun House follow a route through what are in effe
contrasting styles, one designed by Sir William Bruce and the other
both famous Scottish architects. The original Entrance Hall which li
on plan facing p.24) was made more imposing by removing the floor of the room above and
redesigning the Hall to harmonise with the Adam alterations. This work was undertaken
by William Adam's son John in the early 1750s.

The portrait above the chimneypiece is of the 7th Earl of Hopetoun, who was appointed in 1901 to
be the first Governor-General of the Commonwealth of Australia and was created Marquess of
Linlithgow. Opposite is his son, the 2nd Marquess, who was Britain's longest-serving Viceroy of India
(1936-1943). Both wear the robes of Knight of the Thistle. The latter was also created Knight of the
Garter. They were respectively great-grandfather and grandfather of the present Lord Linlithgow.

The white marble chimneypiece with the Apollo head dates from 1754. On either side are marble
busts of Frederick Duke of York and Albany and of the Duke of Wellington, both by the Edinburgh
sculptor Thomas Campbell c. 1827. The white roundels were probably part of the great collection of
classical marbles brought from Italy in 1720 by the 2nd Marquess of Annandale whose sister married
the 1st Earl of Hopetoun. They are inscribed Marcus Cato, Pompeius Magnus, Castracanus and
Hericus. The marble floor was supplied by Jacob Coornhart of Rotterdam in 1753.

PAINTINGS:
On the wall facing the entrance are portraits of *Lord Macdonald of Sleat* by Sir John Watson Gordon and of *Charles Hope, Lord Granton* (1763-1851) Lord President of the Court of Session, great-grandson of the 1st Earl of Hopetoun, painted by Sir Henry Raeburn. Opposite hangs a sabre presented to Lord Granton by his Regiment.

The painting on the adjoining wall is of *King George II at the Battle of Dettingen* and directly opposite is *The Duke of Cumberland at the Battle of Culloden*, both by John Wootton.

FURNITURE:
The furniture includes an Italian console table *c.* 1720 with sample marbles, two marble top console tables by Bossi 1790 and a round table *c.* 1830 in burr oak.

2nd Marquess of Linlithgow by Sir Oswald Birley.

THE LIBRARIES

The libraries, as at present arranged, are an adaptation of several small rooms: formerly bedchamber, drawing-room, dressing-room and closet. Sometime after 1720 when Adam's new plans for the house were published in *Vitruvius Scoticus,* it was proposed to house the library in the new South Pavilion, now occupied by the Ballroom. It is not clear whether this plan was ever effected. Certainly by the early 19th century, the libraries were in their present position.

Many members of the family from John Hope of Hopetoun (1650-1682) to the present day have collected books in Britain and Europe. The Library has many early books on law, philosophy and archaeology. Notable among these are working volumes, bound in vellum, used by young Hopes studying at Leyden and Utrecht Universities in the 17th and 18th centuries. Other books came to the Library after the marriage of Charles, the 1st Earl, to Lady Henrietta Johnstone whose brother, the 2nd Marquess of Annandale, was a noted patron of the arts. 19th century books include poetry, memoirs, European classics, religious commentaries and histories of Europe.

The table holds a display of hand-painted formal addresses, press-cuttings and photographs from the years when the family was in Australia and India.

All of the books undergo a regular programme of cleaning and conservation.

The gilded carving and pilasters seen both in the Small Library and in the Garden Parlour beyond are typical of Bruce's treatment of wainscot (panelling). He was much influenced by buildings he had seen during political excursions to the Netherlands and France.

The screen with flower plates contains illustrations from the *Temple of Flora* by Robert John Thornton who dedicated this work to Queen Charlotte, consort of King George III. Thornton, a Doctor of Medicine, aimed to glorify botany and ally it with 'the pleasing arts of painting and engraving' – to which end he engaged eminent artists to paint the pictures, which were then transferred to copper by more than a dozen engravers. The attributions can be clearly seen on the plates.

Opposite: the Large Library.

Right: the Small Library.

Below: display of illuminated addresses.

PAINTINGS (LARGE LIBRARY):

John Hope of Hopetoun (1650-1682), father of the 1st Earl of Hopetoun. Artist unknown.
Lady Jemima and Lady Lucy Hope, daughters of the 3rd Earl of Hopetoun, by David Allan *c.* 1782.
Major General Sir Alexander Hope (1769-1837), son of the 2nd Earl of Hopetoun, by Sir Thomas Lawrence.
William Pitt (1759-1806), by John Hoppner.

FURNITURE (LARGE LIBRARY):

Early 18th century pier glasses.
Mid-18th century needlework chairs.
Chimney-piece of Glentilt marble.
French slate clock with malachite insets, showing perpetual calendar and thermometers, *c.* 1850.
Early 19th century billiard-table.

PAINTINGS (SMALL LIBRARY):

Jane, Countess of Hopetoun (d. 1767), second wife of the 2nd Earl of Hopetoun (pastel portrait by William Hoare).
Boy with ruff, by Domenico Feti.
Girl with dog, by Lavinia Fontana.
Two portraits of children by Antonio Amorosi.
Lady Henrietta Hope (1746-1786), daughter of the 2nd Earl of Hopetoun (pastel portrait by William Hoare).
Ships Exchanging a Salute, by William van de Velde.
John, 2nd Earl of Hopetoun (1704-1781), (pastel portrait by William Hoare).
Charles, Lord Hope (1740-1766), eldest son of the 2nd Earl of Hopetoun, by Nathaniel Dance.

THE GARDEN PARLOUR

A musical automaton clock by Jan Henkels of Amsterdam, c.1730.

This room gave access to what were once formal gardens laid out on the west lawn leading to the round mirror pond with its jet of water. The patterns of arabesques and shells may occasionally be seen to this day, some 250 years after the style went out of fashion, by noticing the lines of daisies or the greener patches after a dry spell. Good views of the patterns are obtainable from the Roof-top Viewing Platform (see Page 19).

Seen through the centre doors is the early 18th century stone porch supported on each side by twin columns. The masonry of this part of the house was by Tobias Bauchop, of Alloa, who had worked for Bruce at Kinross House and Craigiehall. His account for the years 1702-6 survives in the family papers and amounts to £5,460 Scots (£455 sterling).

The musical automaton clock (left), manufactured by Jan Henkels of Amsterdam *c*.1730 shows the time, day, month, date and phase of the moon, the latter being most important to travellers on the rough tracks of those days and to merchant shippers awaiting high tides. Just before the hour the windmill revolves and the orchestra appears to play a gentle tinkling tune before the clock strikes the hour.

PAINTINGS:

John, 4th Earl of Hopetoun by Sir John Watson Gordon (above chimneypiece). The Earl is wearing the uniform of the Company of Archers of which he was Captain-General in 1822.
The Meeting of Cleopatra and Mark Antony at Tarsus (above coin cabinet) is an early copy of the 1647 painting by Claude Lorraine which hangs in the Louvre.

FURNITURE, etc.:

Side table with marble slab, French *c*. 1700. Set of chairs *c*. 1720 with 19th century needlework.
Folding screen incorporating a series of plates from a 17th century book of horsemanship by the Duke of Newcastle, engraved by Lucas Vorsteman and others. 19th century silver wall sconces. Chimneypiece of Portsoy marble. Iron grate (1704) by William Aitken.

The Writing Closet chimneypiece.

The Charter Room.

THE WRITING CLOSET

Bruce designed corner chimneypieces for some of his smaller rooms and here is a pleasing example. There is another one upstairs. This room was originally the Dressing Room.

ENGRAVINGS:
Roman Ruins by Luigi Rossini (dated 1820-1823). They form part of a collection of prints of the kind which were purchased by Grand Tour travellers.

FURNITURE:
George II mahogany-framed bureau cabinet on bracket feet.

THE CHARTER ROOM

Here we see how provision was made in the 18th century to safeguard the title deeds and family muniments. The original shelving and deed boxes survive and some of the 18th century estate books are displayed, including tack books, rent rolls and domestic accounts.

This small chamber was converted in 1708. It is fireproof with a stone-vaulted ceiling. The heavy iron door and the window were made by William Aitken.

THE BRUCE BEDCHAMBER
(see page 6)

FRONT STAIRS

The staircase is one of the chief decorative features of the Bruce house. The pine-panelled walls, frieze, cornice and panel borders were carved with flowers, fruit, wheatears and peapods by Alexander Eizat, a Scottish woodcarver who had worked with Bruce at Holyrood Palace. The hand-rail and banisters are of oak.

At the foot of the stairs is a longcase clock *c.*1750, signed Andrew Dickie, Edinburgh. Beside it hangs a portrait of Charles, 3rd Marquess of Linlithgow (1912-1987), wearing the uniform of Lord Lieutenant of the County of West Lothian. It was painted by Leonard Boden in 1983.

Tideman's canvases were contained here in the framed panels, but the murals to be seen today are modern, painted in 1967 by the well-known Scottish *trompe l'oeil* artist, William McLaren, who was commissioned by the 3rd Marquess to paint the panels as a memorial to his wife who had died four years earlier. The first panel depicts Lady Linlithgow in the medallion between the sphinxes, here representing Night and Day. Beneath lie a trinket box and a small notebook belonging to her daughter and son. In the next panel, Cupid joins Scotland and England together. Here, and in the succeeding panels, are scenes and small remembrances of Lady Linlithgow and her love for Hopetoun with its variety of wildlife.

The 3rd Marquess by Leonard Boden, 1983 (detail).

THE BRUCE BEDCHAMBER

Sir William Bruce designed this room as the bedchamber of the young 1st Earl in a suite of three rooms comprising bedroom, dressing room and closet. The gilded wall paintings were by the Edinburgh decorator James Norrie in 1741-2 when the room was converted to serve as a small family drawing room.

PAINTINGS:

In 1703 a series of paintings was commissioned for Hopetoun from the artist Philip Tideman (1657-1705) who was working in Amsterdam. The subjects were from Greek mythology to symbolise the virtues and give supposed moral encouragement to the occupants of the rooms. The three overdoor paintings in this room are *The Rewards of Learning*, *The Choice between Virtue and Vice* and *The Patronage of Music*.

FURNITURE:

The gilt four-poster bed, hung with red damask was supplied in 1768 by the workshop of Mathias Lock of London for the Great Bedchamber (now the State Dining Room).

Fine mahogany night table, one of a pair made by James Cullen in 1766 for the Great Bedchamber.

Gilt overmantel mirror *c.* 1740. Gilt pier glass *c.* 1740.

The Pattern Chair is a unique survival. It was made by James Cullen to display various forms of carving to enable the 2nd Earl to select which style he preferred for the State Apartments.

Commode of Spanish mahogany attributed to James Cullen (restored after fire damage).

THE STATE DINING ROOM

This room was created in the early 19th century by the architect James Gillespie Graham who combined the Ante-Chamber and Great Bedchamber. It therefore represents a fine example of a late Regency room as practically everything in it dates from that period, including the cornice decoration, the chimneypiece, elaborate curtains and golden wallpaper.

It was fashionable at the time to have the family portraits hung in the dining room.

FURNITURE:
Mahogany sideboard (c. 1820).
Mahogany dining table (c. 1820).
Gilt pier tables (c. 1820) with 18th century marble slab bearing the cypher of Charles Lord Hope.
Mahogany dining chairs by James Cullen from the original State Dining Room (now the Yellow Drawing Room).
Side tables with marble slabs (c. 1730) perhaps supplied for this room in 1820.

PORCELAIN:
Large Meissen vases decorated with flowers and fruit, early 19th century. Set of dessert plates, French (c. 1820) bearing the Earl's coronet and "H" for Hopetoun. Meissen vase with pierced top (c. 1820). Minton oyster dish. Chinese Canton vases (1830) celadon ground with famille rose decoration. Dresden vases (c. 1820).
Early 20th century candelabra and other table silver of various dates.
Dessert service - Derby (1820).
White wine and port glasses in Edinburgh Crystal of the *Star of Edinburgh* pattern. These are produced at a modern factory by traditional methods.

PAINTINGS:
John, 2nd Earl of Hopetoun – copy by Sir Henry Raeburn from the original by Allan Ramsay.
Charles, 1st Earl of Hopetoun by David Allan (painted posthumously).
Charles, 1st Earl of Hopetoun and *Henrietta, Countess of Hopetoun*, sister of the 2nd Marquess of Annandale – both by William Aikman.
John Hope of Hopetoun (unattributed) and *4th Earl of Seafield* by Sir John Medina.
Sir Thomas Hope, Lord Advocate, by George Jamesone (copy).
Henrietta de Coligny, wife of 3rd Earl of Haddington by unidentified French artist.
Charles Hope Vere by David Allan.
Sir Thomas Hope of Kerse by George Jamesone (copy).
John, 2nd Earl of Hopetoun by Allan Ramsay.
Jane, Countess of Hopetoun by Gainsborough.

Sir James Hope of Hopetoun by George Jamesone (copy).
John, 5th Earl of Hopetoun by Sir John Watson Gordon.
Major General Sir Alexander Hope by Fueger.
The 2nd Marquess of Annandale by Procaccini.
John, 4th Earl of Hopetoun by Sir John Watson Gordon.
The Right Honourable John Hope by Colvin Smith.
Sir Archibald Hope (artist unknown).
Hon. Henry Hope with Dr. Gillies by David Allan.
Colonel John Somerville attributed to J. Ross.

Below left: one of the dining chairs with pine-apple motif.

Below: Jane Countess of Hopetoun by Gainsborough.

The design of the canvas-work chair seats was created from the 'pine-apple' of hospitality surrounded by scrollwork of the type to be seen in the décor of the Yellow Drawing Room, which was the original formal dining room.

The seats were completed in 1989 by a group of volunteers, many of whom are involved throughout the year in the conservation of textiles such as silks and tapestries and in the replacement of hangings.

In addition to these volunteers, there are others who care for the books in the Library, and skilled professionals who maintain the paintings and the ceramics, as well as the fabric of the building.

Whilst in earlier days women would have been kept busy with domestic affairs, Jane Countess of Hopetoun lived in an era when such tasks were delegated to staff. Social life abounded and elegant new crafts were practised, such as the netting at which Gainsborough has captured his sitter, her materials retained in the decorative bag on her arm. Netting, a dainty form of the fisherman's craft, was measured by the gauge which she holds in one hand, and could be accomplished easily while conversation ensued. After sufficient 'framework' had been completed, a form of darning filled in the squares to form a pattern which could be overlaid on brightly-coloured silk.

THE HOPE FAMILY

The Hope family has a long and honourable record of service to crown, country, the law and the sciences. The progenitor of the Hopes of Hopetoun, now represented by the 4th Marquess of Linlithgow, was *John Hope*, a Burgess of Edinburgh, (deceased by 1561), who was at the court of James IV in the late 15th century. The family had merchant trading connections with the continent; one son, *Henry*, (circa 1533-1591), being a burgess of both Dieppe and of Edinburgh. Following the Massacre of St. Bartholomew in 1572, Henry's family settled in Edinburgh, where his son, Thomas was born.

Sir Thomas Hope of Craighall (1573-1646), studied law. Early in his career, his able and brave defence of a Protestant Assembly contrary to Royal edict, brought the young advocate into the public eye. His career advanced, and, like many advocates of his time, he purchased lands. In 1626, Charles I appointed him King's Advocate, an office he held for twenty years. He emerges through the pages of history as a thoroughly trustworthy, kindly family man.

Of his four surviving sons, two became judges at the Court of Session, the third was cup-bearer to the king, and the fourth, *Sir James Hope* (1614-1661), became Master of the Mint and a Lord of Session. He was the first to style himself 'of Hopetoun', using the old name for Leadhills in Lanarkshire where, through his marriage with the heiress, Anne Foulis, he came into possession of valuable lead mines. Sir James travelled to the Low Countries to study mineralogy and brought the art of mining to a perfection hitherto unknown in Scotland. These interests extended into West Lothian in the area of the Bathgate Hills in 1657.

In 1678, his son, *John Hope* (1650-1682), purchased the lands of Abercorn, on which the present house stands, transferring the name "Hopetoun" to his new properties. Sadly, John Hope of Hopetoun was not to see the development of Hopetoun House, as he was drowned in a shipwreck whilst accompanying the Duke of York, later James VII/ II, on a journey to Scotland. John's widow, the beautiful and capable Lady Margaret Hamilton, left with two young children, continued the discussion of plans for erecting a mansion on the present site.

Right: Sir Thomas Hope of Craighall.

Below left: John Hope of Hopetoun.

Below: Charles, 1st Earl of Hopetoun.

Charles Hope (1681-1742) raised to the Peerage as Earl of Hopetoun in 1703, married the sister of the 2nd Marquess of Annandale, a noted connoisseur of the arts with an outstanding collection which on his death came to Hopetoun. Their son, *John, 2nd Earl of Hopetou*n (1704-1781), was involved in the decoration of the State Apartments and was also a noted 'agricultural improver'.

He was also responsible for the purchase of the Ormiston estates in East Lothian which he acquired from John Cockburn (the famous agricultural improver) and was one of the first Governors of Edinburgh Infirmary. *James, the 3rd Earl* (1741-1816), further improved the estates agriculturally. By this time, the family owned large areas in East and West Lothian, Fife and Lanarkshire.

As the 3rd Earl had no son, he was succeeded by his half brother, *General Sir John Hope* (1765-1823), as 4th Earl. He had had a distinguished military career, receiving honours for his outstanding services and bravery. He carried out the evacuation of British troops from Corunna, and fought under Wellington in the Peninsular War. At Hopetoun he was responsible for the completion of the present State Dining Room, and for the purchase of several important pictures in the house. In 1822, he entertained George IV at Hopetoun on the final day of the Royal visit to Scotland.

The 5th and 6th Earls were both active in Scottish affairs and in the improvement of their estates. *John, the 7th Earl* (1860-1908), was one of the most eminent members of the family. After being Governor of Victoria he was made the first Governor-General of the Commonwealth of Australia in 1901. He was created Marquess of Linlithgow. *Victor, the 2nd Marquess* (1887-1952), held the office of Viceroy and Governor-General of India from 1936 to 1943. He had twin sons; the elder, *Charles, the 3rd Marquess* (1912-1987), served in the Army during the war, and was taken prisoner with the 51st (Highland) Division in 1940, finally being held at Colditz as one of the 'prominente'. He and his son Adrian were responsible for the formation of the Hopetoun House Preservation Trust in 1974.

Adrian, the present Marquess (b. 1946), pursued a career in the City of London, but now lives with his family in part of Hopetoun House, from where he supervises the running of the family estates around Hopetoun and at Leadhills, and as a Trustee takes a keen interest in the conservation of his ancestral home for the benefit of visitors from all over the world. He has two sons by his first marriage, *Andrew, Earl of Hopetoun* (b. 1969) and *Lord Alexander* (b. 1971), and, by his second marriage, a daughter, *Lady Louisa* (b. 1981) and a son, *Lord Robert (Bertie)* (b. 1984).

Left: full-length portrait of John, 2nd Earl of Hopetoun in his Parliamentary robes as a Scottish representative peer. The painting is an exact copy by Sir Henry Raeburn of a portrait painted by Allan Ramsay for the Royal Infirmary, Edinburgh to which the sitter had made an endowment. No other Raeburn copy of a Ramsay portrait is known.

Hopetoun by Moonlight.

24